BBC QUIZBOOKS
TELLY ADDICTS

Telly Addicts

compiled by

Tim Manning and Richard Lewis

BBC BOOKS

Telly Addicts was devised
by John King

Published by BBC Books
A division of BBC Enterprises Ltd
Woodlands, 80 Wood Lane, London W12 0TT

First published 1987
Reprinted 1987
© British Broadcasting Corporation 1987
Foreword © Noel Edmonds 1987

ISBN 0 563 20597 0

Photoset by Wilmaset, Birkenhead, Wirral
Printed in Great Britain by
Richard Clay Ltd, Bungay, Suffolk

PREFACE

Dear Patient

The conquest of an addiction owes as much to the recognition of the existence of the addiction as to the actual cause itself. As with dependence upon other stimulants, it is vital that you, the patient, come to terms with the scale of the problem.

Recognising the symptoms of Telly Addiction is difficult because no two cases are the same. However, if your hands shake unless gripping a remote controller, if you arrange meal times to suit the TV schedules, and if you believe Terry Wogan is a real person, you've got it. But do not be alarmed – help is available through that fine medical authority, the BBC. It has been proved that regular exposure to television programmes presented by myself produces a euphoric reaction much appreciated by all addicts. The Pain family from Swindon and the Reynish family of Swansea will testify to the effectiveness of this treatment.

That is the good news. The bad news is that after months of working with these patients I, too, have succumbed to the disease. My case is particularly bad. I always have my little hooferdoofer in my hand and regularly eat from a tray upon my lap. Although for the moment I'm not so sick as to believe that Terry Wogan is a real person.

If you think that *you* have the addiction, may I suggest that you swallow the entire contents of this publication and then write to me for an application form for the next series of *Telly Addicts*.

Best wishes

Dr N. Edmonds

A NOTE BEFORE PLAYING

The questions in this book have been arranged in 14 games, each of 7 rounds. Some rounds are made up of questions to test your knowledge of particular kinds of programmes – westerns or comedies, for example – and others to find out how much you know about a wide range of television. And to add to the fun, you'll see that each game contains a whole page of the *Telly Addicts* favourite, the Props Bag!

With two or more people playing, why not divide the questions in each round between you? But however you play, if you can come up with all the answers, you're a real Telly Addict!

CONTENTS

GAME 1

Round 1: General

1 In which series did Ralph Waite play a river-boat-owning lawyer?

2 What does 'V' stand for and where did they come from?

3 Complete this programme title – *Scarecrow and . . .*

4 Why were Hardcastle and McCormick an odd team?

5 Dirk Benedict and Dwight Schultz are two members of which team?

6 What's the connection between *Bullseye* and *Muck and Brass*?

7 Who plays Nigel Havers' partner in *Don't Wait Up*?

8 Which detective investigated in *Cover Her Face*?

9 Name the science-fiction trilogy scrapped after the second series.

10 Who played Marie Curie?

11 What happened to Danny in the final episode of *Juliet Bravo*?

12 What historical event was the subject of the drama *The Last Place on Earth*?

Round 2: Pop Shows

1　On which show were records voted a hit or miss?

2　Marty Wilde was one of the presenters of what?

3　Who chaired *Pop Quiz*?

4　Complete this programme title – *Lift off with . . .* ?

5　What city did *Top of the Pops* originally come from?

6　Who gave it 'foive'?

7　Name the main presenter of *Revolver*.

8　Who chaired a revived series of *Juke Box Jury*?

9　Wrestling commentator Kent Walton presented a pop show. Name it.

10　Which keyboard musician presented *The Tube*?

11　Which *Open House* disc jockey co-presented *Six-Five Special*?

12　Which pop show is presented by Dave Lee Travis?

Round 3: General

1   What was Alf Garnett renamed in the American remake of *Till Death Us Do Part*?

2   Who was the quizmaster on *Ask The Family*?

3   Which Dr Who hosted *The Book Tower*?

4   Who presents both *Crimewatch UK* and *A Week In Politics*?

5   Who left *Breakfast Time* to be *Game For A Laugh*?

6   In *Bootsie and Snudge*, what was Bootsie's surname?

7   What sort of vehicle did Ironside drive around in?

8   What was *Robin's Nest*?

9   Which series features Manford Safari Park and Bellington Zoo?

10 What's the name of the last-but-one round on *The Price Is Right*?

11 Who is Michael Knight's boss in *Knight Rider*?

12 Which equestrian series was presented by Ian Ogilvy and Lucinda Green?

From these lists of props identify a television character:

1   a A pair of ankle socks.
    b A wrap-around overall.
    c A trolley laden with polish, dusters, mops and
      buckets.

2   a A set of morning papers.
    b A blazer with military badges on its pocket.
    c A hotel-room key.

3   a A butler's outfit.
    b A pink Rolls-Royce.
    c A chauffeur's hat.

4   a A large block of ice.
    b A man's black cape.
    c A walking stick concealing a sword.

5   a A police identity card.
    b A map of Jersey.
    c A vintage car.

6   a A bowler hat.
    b A pair of small round glasses.
    c An army captain's tunic.

What animals are these puppet characters?

1 Parsley.

2 Dillon.

3 Kermit.

4 Sage.

5 Rag, Tag and Bobtail.

6 Soo.

7 Basil Brush.

8 Kevin.

9 Ermintrude.

10 Pinky and Perky.

11 Pongo.

12 Prudence.

Round 6: General

1 Who hosts *That's my Dog*?

2 Who forsook CB TV for a weekly helicopter ride?

3 Who was the star of *The History Man*?

4 Who supplied Margaret Thatcher's voice for *Spitting Image*?

5 What is *Wonder Woman*'s proper title?

6 In *Kung Fu* what did the old priest call the young boy?

7 Who worked for Nemesis?

8 The USS *Enterprise* belongs to the fleet of which organisation?

9 Which company did Sir John Wilder aim to control?

10 Which actress ran The Flying Swan?

11 Who was killed in a siege in Brookside Close?

12 Who plays Sergeant Jablonski in *Hill Street Blues*?

Identify the jobs or occupations of the following
TV characters:

1   Den Watts.

2   Bill Brand.

3   Harold Steptoe.

4   John Watt.

5   Danny McGlone.

6   April Dancer.

7   Harry McSween.

8   Romana.

9   Heather Haversham.

10   Bernard Hedges.

11   Hilary.

12   Roland Rat.

GAME 2

Round 1: General

1 Who plays Valene in *Knots Landing*?

2 Who did George Layton play in *It Ain't Half Hot, Mum*?

3 Who played 'Medallion Man' in *Three of a Kind*?

4 Which *That's Life* presenter wrote the theme song to *The Marriage*?

5 Whose other catchprase is – '. . . and you may answer'?

6 In which soap did Lane Ballou play the piano at Lute Mae's?

7 What did Roy Plomley ask celebrities to talk about on TV?

8 Who's the 'whispering' snooker commentator?

9 Who was Jim Bergerac's father-in-law?

10 What do losing contestants take home on *Blankety Blank*?

11 Name the sit-com that starred Edward Woodward and Hilary Tyndall?

12 According to the side of Del Boy's three-wheeler, where do the Trotters have offices?

Round 2: Mini-Series

1 In which mini-series did Pamela Sue Martin and Patrick Duffy co-star?

2 Which writer adapted *Tender is the Night* for television?

3 Who played President Monckton in *Washington Behind Closed Doors*?

4 Who created *Lace*?

5 Which famous Hollywood star played a 'madam' in *North and South*?

6 In which horrific mini-series did James Mason play a sinister role?

7 What was the title of the mini-series about the perfume business?

8 Who played Evita Peron?

9 In *Return to Eden*, who played Dan?

10 Which Hollywood star narrated *Shogun*?

11 In which mini-series did Stacey Keach play a painter?

12 Who was the Irish builder in *A Woman of Substance*?

1 Where did Alexis marry Cecil?

2 Who was thawed out to solve crimes in the sixties?

3 Who wrote *Barmitzvah Boy*?

4 Richard Beckinsale and Paula Wilcox were what?

5 Who said '*Can We Talk?*'?

¾ Who played Mr Rose?

7 What did *Not the Nine O'Clock News* and *Muck and Brass* have in common?

8 In which hospital would you find the *Young Doctors*?

9 Who was the resident singer on *Carrott Confidential*?

10 Who was *Edna, The Inebriate Woman*?

11 What happened if you said Yes or No to Michael Miles?

12 Who did B.J. replace?

Round 4: Props Bag

From these lists of props identify a television character:

1 a A tin of damp proofing.
   b A rent book.
   c An old cardigan.

2 a A set of false eyelashes.
   b A blonde wig.
   c A pair of stilettos with broken-down heels.

3 a A gavel.
   b A white bow tie.
   c A dictionary.

4 a A Mercedes car.
   b A stetson.
   c A membership card for The Cattlemen's Club.

5 a A set of valves.
   b A blue transit van.
   c A half of bitter.

6 a An army cap badge.
   b A large sign that says 'QUIET!'
   c A list of new recruits.

In which towns and cities are the following series set?

1 *Bread.*

2 *Kojak.*

3 *Juliet Bravo.*

4 *Van Der Valk.*

5 *Z Cars.*

6 *Casualty.*

7 *Gangsters.*

8 *Boys from the Black Stuff.*

9 *All Creatures Great and Small.*

10 *Dr Finlay's Casebook.*

11 *Mapp and Lucia.*

12 *Fawlty Towers.*

1 Where would you find 'Bully'?

2 Sharon and Elsie worked in the office of what kind of factory?

3 Who presented *The Fame Game*?

4 Which actress might have said '*That's My Boy*'?

5 Who wrote *The Mistress*?

6 Name the two stars of *Roll Over Beethoven*.

7 Which group celebrated a silver anniversary in *Tutti Frutti*?

8 Who played Blott?

9 What did Radar O'Reilly sleep with?

10 Name the host of *Babble*.

11 Who played the two girls in *Man About the House*?

12 What job did Robert Gillespie do in *Keep It In The Family*?

Round 7: Wildlife

1   Who hosts the *Really Wild Show*?

2   Which wildlife quiz was chaired by Henry Kelly?

3   Which married couple were famous on TV safaris in the 1950s?

4   Which wildlife film-maker brought you his *Country Diary*?

5   Who went on a *Zoo Quest*?

6   Who presents *Animals Roadshow*?

7   In which series did David Attenborough have close encounters with gorillas?

8   Who took you on a *Backyard Safari*?

9   Who is the host of the BBC's live *Birdwatch* programmes?

10   Which husband and wife team pioneered undersea film-making for television?

11   Who brought you his *World of Flowers*?

12   Who would show you his *Undersea World*?

GAME 3

1   In *Moonlighting*, what is the name of the detective agency?

2   Who plays *The District Nurse*?

3   What is the name of Dr Who's grand-daughter?

4   Who runs the post office in *Postman Pat*?

5   If Hector was a dog, what was Kiki?

6   What was the name of the pet alien in *Fireball XL5*?

7   In which comedy series did Derek Nimmo play a monk?

8   Which drama series featured the Hammond family?

9   Who presented *Civilisation*?

10 Who played Skullion in *Porterhouse Blue*?

11 What is the more familiar name of *Jeux Sans Frontières*?

12 What was the name of the female baddie in *Blake's Seven*?

Round 2: Talk Shows

1 On which show did Gilbert Harding break down and cry?

2 Which former *News At Ten* newsreader presents a daytime show?

3 Name Terry Wogan's early evening weekend show.

4 Who interviews *One to One*?

5 Which British talk show host scooped an interview with Richard Nixon?

6 Whose twice-weekly chat shows came from Manchester and London?

7 Who jumped into a white sports car at the end of his show?

8 Bernard Falk presented a late-night series on what subject?

9 Which lyricist presented his own chat show?

10 Jonathon Ross presents what?

11 What was Derek Nimmo's chat show called?

12 Name the daytime phone-in show that looks at TV.

Round 3: General

1　Who is the history teacher at Hardwicke House?

2　Which family was the Fonz friendly with?

3　Which husband and wife team star in *My Husband and I*?

4　Name Channel 4's Sunday-morning Asian soap opera.

5　Who hosts *People Do The Funniest Things*?

6　What kind of phrase does Roy Walker like to hear?

7　Who presents ITN's *News At One*?

8　Who are Wesley and Cyril?

9　What are Fitz and John?

10　What sort of shop does Bulman work from?

11　In *Bewitched* who is Darrin's mother-in-law?

12　Who plays Max Headroom?

From these lists of props identify a television character:

1 a A long red wig.
    b A clipboard marked 'Eagle Television'.
    c A tin of bird seed.

2 a A large thumb.
    b A dressing gown.
    c A map of the universe.

3 a An astronaut's helmet.
    b A green bottle.
    c A book of magic spells.

4 a A Jaguar car.
    b A wedding ring – still in its box.
    c A plastic cigarette.

5 a A cigar butt.
    b A fisherman's hat covered in 'flies'.
    c A surgeon's mask.

6 a A wrap-around apron.
    b A set of curlers.
    c A pair of wrinkled stockings.

Round 5: Arts and Science

1 Who hosted *Aquarius*?

2 Who wrote the signature tune of *The South Bank Show*?

3 Which former newsreader introduces *The Last Night of the Proms*?

4 Who was the original host of *Tomorrow's World*?

5 In which series did Margaret Thatcher do experiments in the kitchen?

6 Where are the headquarters of the Open University?

7 Which famous broadcaster was associated with *Monitor*?

8 Which controversial film-director made a film about Elgar for *Monitor*?

9 Who introduces *The South Bank Show*?

10 In which series about variety did Roy Hudd visit theatres across Britain?

11 Which arts magazine is hosted by Russell Davies?

12 Which arts series features a floating bottle in its title sequence?

Round 6: General

1 Who played Lord Brett Sinclair?

2 What line of business was Lovejoy involved in?

3 What's the connection between *Z Cars* and *One By One*?

4 Where would you find Karl Malden and Michael Douglas?

5 Who's the barman at the Winchester Club?

6 Which actress played Thelma in *The Likely Lads*?

7 What's the registration number of Bergerac's car?

8 In *Only Fools and Horses*, what was Uncle Albert's naval rank?

9 Who was the first host of *A Question of Sport*?

10 Which quiz does Angela Rippon host?

11 Who played Eric Sykes's sister?

12 Who wrote *Steptoe and Son*?

Which sports were associated with these series?

1 *Give Us A Break.*

2 *Eh Brian It's a Whopper.*

3 *Driving Ambition.*

4 *Jossy's Giants.*

5 *Tales from the Longroom.*

6 *The Challenge.*

7 *United.*

8 *Bodyline.*

9 *Howards' Way.*

10 *Murphy's Mob.*

11 *Follyfoot.*

12 *Charters and Caldicott.*

GAME 4

1 What did Morticia Addams do to roses?

2 Who is the regular host of Channel 4's *Right to Reply*?

3 Who married George Dixon's daughter?

4 What was the title of the original theme of *BBC Television News*?

5 Who narrates *The Wind in the Willows*?

6 Where was Napoleon Solo's two-way radio?

7 What was the name of the hotel in *The Duchess of Duke Street*?

8 Which husband and wife team played a chauffeur and a maid in *Upstairs Downstairs*?

9 How did Toby Wren die?

10 What was the name of the hospital where Dr Kildare worked?

11 What was Jim Rockford's phone number?

12 Who only came out to play when Andy and Teddy weren't around?

Round 2: News and Newsreaders

1 Which former BBC newsreader has become a popular weekend chat show host?

2 Who lost a tooth while reading the news?

3 Which early ITN newscaster was also an accomplished athlete?

4 Which *News At Ten* newscaster went on to become a very fashionable presenter?

5 Who is the main presenter of Channel 4 *News*?

6 Which TV newsreader showed her legs to Morecambe and Wise?

7 Which clock is featured in the opening titles of *News At Ten*?

8 Which award-winning BBC reporter covered the American bombing of Tripoli in 1986?

9 Which ITN newscaster risked danger to make a series of films in Afghanistan?

10 Which breakfast newsreader is also a thriller writer?

11 Who retired from newsreading, and went on to front *Years Ahead*?

12 Who left ITN to present the BBC's *News At One*?

Round 3: General

1 What was the name of the band in *Rock Follies*?

2 Which family owned the homestead where Shane lived?

3 Which former *Breakfast Time* financial expert hosts *Money Spinner*?

4 In *To The Manor Born*, what sort of business was De Vere in?

5 What sort of dragon was featured in *Clangers*?

6 Who played Fleur in *The Forsyte Saga*?

7 Name the Royalist family in *By the Sword Divided*.

8 Name the character played by Maureen Lipman in *Agony*.

9 What was the title of the BBC drama series based on the work of the Samaritans?

10 Which magazine did Ian Harman edit?

11 Who was the original host of *Crackerjack*?

12 Name the sci-fi comic strip featured in *Blue Peter* in the 1960s.

From these lists of props identify a television character:

1 a A set of false teeth.
  b A pair of mittens.
  c A battered black Homburg.

2 a A book of bad jokes.
  b A pair of roller skates.
  c A small trilby hat.

3 a A suitcase full of watches.
  b A large bottle of Brut aftershave.
  c A three-wheel car.

4 a A black and white cat.
  b A peaked cap.
  c A post van.

5 a A fat cigar.
  b A pair of pince nez.
  c A powdered wig.

6 a A set of playing cards.
  b A pair of dark-rimmed glasses.
  c An American Army shirt with Master
    Sergeant's stripes.

Round 5: *Crossroads*

1 What was Kath Fellowes' previous married name?

2 Who played Miranda Pollard?

3 Who was the motel's original cleaner?

4 What was Sam Benson's job?

5 Which 'silly ass' became the motel's assistant manager?

6 In which year did Benny first appear in Crossroads?

7 What was the name of Jill Chance's brother?

8 Which fictional Birmingham suburb is featured in the series?

9 Who is Margaret Grice's mother?

10 What was the name of the postman in the early days of the series?

11 Who does Terence Rigby play?

12 What is the name of Tommy's daughter?

1 Which adventure series stars David Hasselhoff?

2 Who presents the sixth-formers' quiz *Connections*?

3 In which comedy series would you find Dr Sheinfeld?

4 What was the nickname of the boss of *WKRP*?

5 Who lived at Arden House?

6 Which comedy series features Simon Peel and Oliver Smallbridge?

7 Which current affairs programme described itself as 'the window on the world'?

8 In Mary, Mungo and Midge, who or what was Midge?

9 What was the title of the original signature tune of *Nationwide*?

10 Who kept the Woodentops' house clean?

11 What relation was Noggin the Nog to Nogbad the Bad?

12 What quiz did Ethel host at *No. 73*?

Round 7: Families

1   Which family featured in *Upstairs Downstairs*?

2   In which daytime soap would you meet the Ramsays?

3   Which family struck oil and moved to Beverly Hills?

4   Which family is featured in *Bewitched*?

5   Mary Beth, Harvey and Harvey Jnr are members of which family?

6   Lou is the matriarch of which family?

7   Which family were runaway winners of the first series of *Telly Addicts*?

8   Which family features in *Family Ties*?

9   In which comedy series would you find the Lumsdens?

10   In which comedy series would you have found the Starlings?

11   Name the one-parent family in *Me and My Girl*?

12   In which comedy series would you find the Trotters?

GAME 5

1   In *Hill Street Blues*, who was Joe Coffey's female patrol partner?

2   In which comedy series does Richard Briers play a vicar?

3   Name the family-owned newspaper in *Chateauvallon*.

4   In *Moonlighting* who did Miss Dipesto fall in love with?

5   What kind of calendar does Hannah Gordon present?

6   Which actor and actress travelled through time and space, but ended up on *Emmerdale Farm*?

7   What does *Y.E.S.* stand for?

8   Name the law firm in *L.A. Law*.

9   In which car would you find Toody and Muldoon?

10 Who hosts *Weekend World*?

11 Name the Boswells' dog, in *Bread*.

12 In *Dad's Army*, what did Corporal Jones do for a living?

Round 2: *Dallas*

1. Name Charlie's pony.
2. Who is Sue Ellen's business partner?
3. Whose sister was a concert pianist?
4. How did Pam and Cliff's mother die?
5. What car does J.R. drive?
6. Who was Sue Ellen's toy boy?
7. Name Jason Ewing's children.
8. What is Cliff Barnes's favourite food?
9. Who claimed to be Jock Ewing?
10. Name Clayton's son.
11. Which character did John Beck play?
12. Who was Ray Krebbs accused of unlawfully killing?

Round 3: General

1 Who was musical director on the *Parkinson* shows?

2 What were Robert Wagner, Jack Hedley and David McCallum trying to escape from?

3 Who was *Richard the Lionheart*?

4 Name the two male occupants of 23 Railway Cuttings, East Cheam.

5 What did *Survivors* survive?

6 What did Simon Templar look up to see at the beginning of each programme?

7 A Rod Stewart recording was used as the theme for which documentary series?

8 Bruce had Anthea, who did Larry have?

9 Who played the original *Pig in the Middle*?

10 What made *The Champions* special?

11 Which war did *Wings* deal with?

12 Name the American newscaster who was commentator on *The Untouchables*.

Round 4: Props Bag

From these lists of props identify a television programme:

1   a A plastic cup.
     b A grey toupee.
     c A pair of glasses.

2   a A baby's bottle.
     b Two handbags.
     c A New York Police Department 'shield'.

3   a A joke book.
     b A motorist's atlas of the UK.
     c A Liverpool Football Club scarf.

4   a A school bell.
     b A road sign – Fenn Street.
     c A school register.

5   a A combat jacket.
     b A suitcase.
     c A three-wheel car.

6   a A jar of curried peaches.
     b A moped.
     c A library ticket.

Round 5: American Soaps

1 What's the nearest town to Southfork?

2 Where did we meet Titus Semple, Claude Weldon, Lane Ballou and Lute Mae Saunders?

3 Name Ryan O'Neal's character in *Peyton Place*.

4 Which spin-off series from *Dallas* features a Ewing?

5 Who was the original Fallon in *Dynasty*?

6 Where did we first meet Lou Grant?

7 Who shot J.R.?

8 Robert Mitchum played 'Pug' Henry in what?

9 Which soap stars the ex-wife of an American president?

10 Name the two Hollywood film stars who were bought to launch *Dynasty II – The Colbys*.

11 Name the characters who forged a horse-breeding partnership in *Dallas*.

12 Which English actor played Blake Carrington's father?

1   Name the TV playwright responsible for *Pennies from Heaven*.

2   Which British daytime drama tried 'cases' on TV in the 1970s?

3   Who chaired *Jokers Wild*?

4   Who went off in *Hannibal's Footsteps*?

5   Name the presenter of *Entertainment USA*.

6   What was Metal Mickey?

7   In which sit-com did we first meet Lewis Collins?

8   Who was *A Married Man*?

9   Cameron Mitchell played which character in *The High Chaparral*?

10 Which lawyer was often seen building his own house?

11 Name the actor who played Quentin Crisp in *The Naked Civil Servant*.

12 Who played Pope Rodrigo Borgia in *The Borgias*?

Round 7: Cowboys

1 Name the ranch run by Big John Cannon.

2 Who was the marshal in *Gunsmoke*?

3 Chuck Connors played a disgraced soldier in which show?

4 Who was *The Virginian*?

5 Name the three Cartwright brothers.

6 Who sang the theme song for *Rawhide*?

7 The Lone Ranger rode Silver; name Tonto's horse.

8 Which two actors played Hannibal Hayes in *Alias Smith and Jones*?

9 Name the Hollywood star who began his career in *Wanted Dead or Alive*.

10 Who were the two Maverick brothers and who played them?

11 Name the character played by Ward Bond in *Wagon Train*.

12 In which show was the dog the hero at Fort Apache?

GAME 6

1   Who was *Foxy Lady*?

2   Oliver Tobias played which British king?

3   What did Jason King do for a living?

4   Who was *The Expert*?

5   Which husband and wife team had *A Fine Romance*?

6   Who drove the Cannon Ball Express?

7   Gene Barry played a millionaire detective in what?

8   In which series was Stephanie Beacham involved in the rag trade?

9   Which band leader began his shows with the cry 'Wakey, wakey!'?

10 In *Cover Up*, what were the fashion photographer and her model supposed to be?

11 Who captained the *Calypso*?

12 Who was *Casanova '73*?

Round 2: Children's Programmes

1 In which show did Johnny Morris appear as a zoo keeper?

2 Christopher Trace and Valerie Singleton presented what?

3 'The Tinder Box' and 'The Singing Ringing Tree' were what?

4 Who presented *Z Shed*?

5 Name the tortoise who was friendly with Bill and Ben.

6 Whose headquarters was a London bus?

7 Witchypoo was the baddie in what?

8 Name the squirrel keen on road safety.

9 Who presented *Zoo Time*?

10 Which ship did Captain Pugwash sail?

11 Bobby Bennett introduced which variety show?

12 Chris Kelly hosted which film review for kids?

Round 3: General

1   Which cartoon character was foiled by Vince and Musky?

2   Who's the char at Acorn Antiques?

3   Frank Muir and Patrick Campbell were the original team captains on which programme?

4   In which programme did Patrick Duffy have webbed feet?

5   Name the family who lived in *The Little House on the Prairie*.

6   Which club did Robbie Box win and what did he rename it?

7   What did USAF Captain Tony Nelson find in a strange green bottle?

8   Which actor originally starred as Wendy Craig's husband in *Not in Front of the Children*?

9   What was the full title of Noel Edmonds's Saturday-morning show for kids?

10 Who was Hughie Green's assistant on *Double Your Money*?

11 Name the talent show hosted by Steve Jones.

12 Which soap opera followed the fortunes of a football team?

From these lists of props identify a television character:

1.   a A battered trilby.
   b Some straw.
   c A turnip.

2.   a A shooting stick.
   b A tweed jacket.
   c A country house.

3.   a A German private's uniform.
   b An oil painting.
   c A casket of gold.

4.   a A monocle.
   b A 1920s car.
   c A copy of *Crime Detection*.

5.   a A dog lead.
   b A ginger wig.
   c A tea cup.

6.   a A policeman's hat.
   b A desk sergeant's diary.
   c A copy of *The Irish Times*.

Round 5: *Dr Who*

1 Which planet did the Daleks come from?

2 Which of the doctor's enemies comes from Mars?

3 What are Dr Who's favourite sweets?

4 What was Bessie?

5 What were the first names of the doctor's first two human companions?

6 What musical instrument did the doctor play?

7 What sort of screwdriver does the doctor use?

8 What's the connection between the doctor and the Valeyard?

9 When the doctor met the Voords what was he searching for?

10 On which planet did the Zarbi live?

11 Which *Blue Peter* presenter was one of the doctor's assistants?

12 Name the doctor's electronic dog.

1 Which *Compact* star went on to run a French café?

2 Where was Dr Zachary Smith?

3 Which Angel became an Eastender?

4 Name Harry Secombe's Sunday-evening programme.

5 Who adapted *Brideshead Revisited* from Evelyn Waugh's novel?

6 In which series did Anthony Andrews defuse bombs?

7 What did Harry Worth do in a shop doorway?

8 Who or what was the other Basil at Fawlty Towers?

9 Which actor appeared with Roger Whittaker in *Whistle Stop* and is now an *'Allo 'Allo!* regular?

10 In which series did a housewife become a rally driver?

11 Name the Ewing family's lawyer.

12 Which oil company was featured in *The Troubleshooters*?

Round 7: *Coronation Street*

1 Who had a cat called Bobby?

2 What was the name of the Hewitts' daughter?

3 How did Ken Barlow's first wife die?

4 Who was the second owner of the corner shop?

5 Who nearly married Leonard Swindley?

6 Which building did Ena Sharples look after?

7 Who was Deirdre Barlow's first husband?

8 How did Ernest Bishop die?

9 Which *Coronation Street* actress used to be a dance band singer?

10 What did Elsie Tanner leave the street to do?

11 Who played Stan Ogden?

12 Which brewery runs the Rovers Return?

GAME 7

1 Who produced *That Was The Week That Was*?

2 Who said 'Woe, woe and thrice woe' and in what?

3 Which American hunk plays *Magnum*?

4 Who asked youngsters to 'think of a number'?

5 Who's chief engineer on the starship *Enterprise*?

6 What does Trigger call Rodney in *Only Fools and Horses*?

7 What was the Clangers' favourite food?

8 Who did the cooking for the Wombles?

9 Who did Howard Hesseman play in *WKRP in Cincinnati*?

10 Who was the rat who helped save a sinking ship?

11 In the series *Phyllis*, who played the title role?

12 In *The Addams Family*, what happened when Uncle Fester put a light bulb in his mouth?

1 Who played *The Secret Servant*?

2 Who was *The Detective*?

3 What was Smiley's first name?

4 Who did Leo G. Caroll play in *The Man from UNCLE*?

5 What was central to the plot of *Bird of Prey*?

6 Stefanie Powers and Noel Harrison starred in which spy spoof?

7 Who played Guy Burgess in *An Englishman Abroad*?

8 Which group had a hit record with the theme from *Harry's Game*?

9 In which jokey thriller series did James Bolam play a schoolteacher?

10 What was Jason King's nom-de-plume?

11 In which series did the two heroes break into 'Northmore'.

12 Who played *Danger Man*?

1   What sort of vehicle did Herman Munster drive?

2   Who was television's *Galloping Gourmet*?

3   What's the connection between *Mr Magoo* and *Gilligan's Island*?

4   In which national park do Yogi Bear and Boo Boo live?

5   Who did Tattoo work for on *Fantasy Island*?

6   In *Tenko*, who played Joss Holbrook?

7   Name the flesh-eating plant featured in *The Addams Family*.

8   In *Dynasty*, which ranch did Sammy-Jo inherit?

9   Name the pub in *Emmerdale Farm*.

10   Name the three men who presented *The Generation Game*.

11   Who was Wogan's first holiday stand-in?

12   Who is Katerina Imperiali di Francabilla better known as?

Round 4: Props Bag

From these lists of props identify a television programme:

1 a A tortoise.
   b A weed.
   c A garden-spade.

2 a An empty cheque book.
   b A map of Oxford.
   c A professor's hat and gown.

3 a A bed pan.
   b A copy of some sheet music from the 1930s.
   c A gold cigarette lighter.

4 a A pair of headphones.
   b A sketchpad.
   c A 'Radio West' programme schedule.

5 a A match.
   b A pipe.
   c A map of Paris.

6 a A blue transit van.
   b A map of Scotland.
   c An electric guitar.

1. Who invited contestants to *Double Your Money*?

2. Name the original host of *Mr and Mrs*.

3. Who were the two 'voice-over' men on *Celebrity Squares*?

4. Which comedian/singer took over *Family Fortunes* from Bob Monkhouse?

5. Steve Race chairs which music quiz?

6. Gilbert Harding and Isobel Barnett were regulars on which show?

7. Where would you be asked specialist and general knowledge questions?

8. Which zany comedian presented *Get Set Go*?

9. Name Bob's 'Golden Girl' on *The Golden Shot*.

10. What could you do if you *didn't* 'open the box'?

11. Who hosted *Punchlines*?

12. What was billed as 'the quiz of the week'?

1 What is Jasper Carrott's real name?

2 Who played Budgie's wife?

3 How many actresses have played Cagney in *Cagney and Lacey*?

4 In which series would you find Cosmo and Dibs?

5 Who owned the house where Dill and Parsley lived?

6 Name the firemen in *Trumpton*.

7 In *The Magic Roundabout*, how did Mr Rusty travel around?

8 Who used 'jaunting' to travel through time and space?

9 Who did Richard Basehart play in *Voyage to the Bottom of the Sea*?

10 Who were Troy Tempest's scaly underwater enemies?

11 In *The Power Game*, what was the name of John Wilder's wife?

12 Who played Petruchio in the BBC TV Shakespeare production of *The Taming of the Shrew*?

Name the actors who appeared as these medical men and women:

1 Dr Cameron.

2 Dr Kildare.

3 Quincy.

4 Dr Stephen Daker.

5 Dr Rose-Marie.

6 Major Frank Burns.

7 Dr Gillespie.

8 Dr Emlyn Isaacs.

9 Dr Andrew Manson.

10 Captain B. J. Hunnicut.

11 Dr Finlay.

12 Marcus Welby M.D.

GAME 8

1 Name the 'switchboard' girl who called up celebrities on *Picture Page*.

2 Who were Bernard Braden's assistants on *The Braden Beat*?

3 What's the connection between *Circus Boy* and *The Rockford Files*?

4 Frank Middlemass played which character in *To Serve Them All My Days*?

5 Who was the long standing (or sitting) chairman of *The Good Old Days*?

6 Name the two comedians who presented *The Wheel Tappers and Shunters Social Club*.

7 Who played Chicken George in *Roots*?

8 Name the series in which Peter Bowles played a gossip columnist.

9 Who was the cockney char who inherited a controlling interest in a business empire?

10 Alec McCowen played *Mr Palfrey of* . . . where?

11 Bernard Hill went on *A Journey in the life of* . . . who?

12 Name Benny Hill's troupe of girls.

Round 2: British Soaps

1 What was the series based around a women's magazine?

2 Name Tom Howard's children.

3 Who played John Wilder in *The Power Game*?

4 Which star of *The Brothers* ended up at *Crossroads*?

5 Which character did Margot Bryant play in *Coronation Street*?

6 Name the hospital where we first met the *Angels*.

7 Which ward dealt with emergencies in the 1950s and 1960s?

8 Which local football team does Arthur follow in *Eastenders*?

9 Who was the *Newcomer* who turned up in *Coronation Street*?

10 Name Frazer Hines's character in *Emmerdale Farm*.

11 Where is Brookside Close?

12 What do Roley and Willie have in common?

Round 3: General

1 Name the two actresses who played the central role in *A Woman of Substance*.

2 Who was Donna Krebbs' baby named after?

3 Whose car did Starsky and Hutch drive around in?

4 What nationality was Van Der Valk?

5 What was Perry Mason's job?

6 Who presented a series sub-titled *Living with Uncle Sam*?

7 Phil Drabble and Eric Halsall present what?

8 Which 'whispering' DJ originally presented *The Old Grey Whistle Test*?

9 Which flamboyant DJ originally presented *Top of the Pops*?

10 Ian Ogilvy 'returned' as what?

11 Who played television's *Odd Couple*?

12 What might Bernard Falk have said to two teams of adventurers?

From these lists of props identify a television character:

1. a A pair of sunglasses.
   b An NYPD cop's shield.
   c A lollipop.

2. a A battered car.
   b A cigar stub.
   c A tatty raincoat.

3. a A pair of pince nez.
   b A bag of knitting.
   c A lady's tweed suit.

4. a A white stetson.
   b A silver bullet.
   c A black eye-mask.

5. a A bright red lipstick.
   b A pair of high heels.
   c A bottle of gin.

6. a A woolly hat.
   b A ferret.
   c A pair of wellies.

Name the sports most associated with these TV commentators:

1 Dan Maskall.

2 David Coleman.

3 Barry Davies.

4 Clive Everton.

5 Tony Green.

6 Raymond Brookes-Ward.

7 Alan Parry.

8 Kent Walton.

9 Sid Waddel.

10 Ron Pickering.

11 Bill McLaren.

12 Brian Moore.

Round 6: General

1 Who introduced *Great Mysteries* in a fedora and cape?

2 Which quiz show was originally part of Thames TV's *Wednesday Night Out*?

3 Name the three actors who played *The Protectors*.

4 Which *Mystery Movie* series starred Rock Hudson and Susan St James?

5 Name the two presenters of *The Clothes Show*.

6 Which former Hollywood actress played a policewoman on TV?

7 What did Kenny Everett do to Terry Wogan's microphone?

8 Name Paul Daniels' first quiz show for BBC TV.

9 Where did we first meet the Osmonds?

10 Max Robertson refereed a contest between experts and collectors – name the programme.

11 Complete this programme title: *Paint with . . .*

12 How did Jock Ewing die?

Round 7: American Comedy

1 Where would you find Sam and Diane in a bar?

2 Who played Little Louie in *Taxi*?

3 Name the US Cavalry comedy that starred Forrest Tucker.

4 Which family became *The Beverly Hillbillies*?

5 What was strange about Max Klinger?

6 Whose boss did Gale Gordon play?

7 Who played Benson?

8 What job does Alice do?

9 What did Samantha and Tabitha have that Darrin didn't?

10 What was Colonel Hall's command?

11 Which show depicted life in an American radio station?

12 Who played Rob Petrie and what did he do for a living?

GAME 9

1 Which quiz show was hosted by George Layton?

2 Which little creatures are always building things in *Fraggle Rock*?

3 Which school featured in *From The Top*?

4 Which international terrorist and revolutionary kidnapped Jessica Tate?

5 Who does Edward Woodward play in *The Equaliser*?

6 In which comedy series did Pat Phoenix play opposite Prunella Gee?

7 In which house would you find Harry, Dawn and Kim?

8 In *Dynasty*, whose sister is Caress?

9 In *Coronation Street*, what happened to David Barlow?

10 In which detective series would you find Spikings?

11 Which children's series features Bork, Drutt and Boni?

12 What does the C.A.T.S. in *C.A.T.S. Eyes* stand for?

1 Who was the song and dance man who starred with Robert Wagner in *It Takes a Thief*?

2 Who played Inspector Lockhart in *No Hiding Place*?

3 What do the actresses Anna Carteret and Stephanie Turner have in common?

4 Who played Andy in *Dixon of Dock Green*?

5 When John Thaw was Regan, who was Dennis Waterman?

6 Which sleuth does Joan Hickson portray?

7 Who played the policeman pursuing David Janssen in *The Fugitive*?

8 Robert Stack was Eliot Ness – in what?

9 On which island did Dano 'book 'em'?

10 In which series would you have found Fancy Smith?

11 Which Latin American crime fighter kept a cockatoo?

12 'Ten Four' was a phrase much used by Broderick Crawford in what?

1 By what name was Steve Austin better known?

2 Who provided Lamb Chop's voice?

3 What job did Serpico do?

4 Burgess Meredith played the head of Probe – in what?

5 Who's missing from this list: Freddy, Daphne, Velma, Shaggy, . . .

6 Who played George Lincoln Rockwell in *Roots: The Next Generations*?

7 'Tomkinson's Schooldays', 'The Curse of the Claw' and 'Murder at Moorstones Manor' were all what?

8 Name Peter Vaughan's character in *Porridge*.

9 Whom did Galen befriend?

10 In *Pennies from Heaven* what did Arthur Parker do for a living?

11 Who was Perry Mason's secretary?

12 Shirley Jones, Suzanne Crough, David Cassidy and Susan Dey were all members of what?

From these lists of props identify a television character:

1 a A pair of boxing gloves.
   b A Capri.
   c A membership card for the Winchester Club.

2 a A large pair of boots.
   b Torn trousers.
   c A six-pack of lager.

3 a A grey trilby.
   b A pair of small round glasses.
   c A West Ham Football Club scarf.

4 a A tennis racquet.
   b A 78 gramophone record.
   c A yellow coat.

5 a A cigar stub.
   b A pair of pince nez.
   c A barrister's wig.

6 a A combat jacket.
   b A card table.
   c A yellow three-wheel car.

Round 5: Costume Drama

1 Who played the king in *The Six Wives of Henry VIII*?

2 Name Eric Porter's character in *The Forsyte Saga*?

3 Gemma Jones was the Duchess of what?

4 Which lusty character did Frank Finlay portray in 1971?

5 Name the series about an eighteenth-century Cornish squire played by Robin Ellis.

6 Who played *Elizabeth R*?

7 Who played *Edward the Seventh*?

8 Where did the Bellamy family live in *Upstairs Downstairs*?

9 Who played Nicholas in Channel 4's production of the RSC's *Nicholas Nickleby*?

10 Who was Pierre in the BBC's adaptation of *War and Peace*?

11 Which Japanese saga starred Richard Chamberlain?

12 Caesare, Lucrecia and Rodrigo shared a family name that was a series title. What is it?

Round 6: General

1 Where did the BBC's first television broadcasts come from?

2 Who was the first regular woman newsreader?

3 On whose show did Frank Bough, Eddie Waring and Barry Norman sing *There is nothing like a dame*?

4 Who played Natalie in Fay Weldon's *Heart of the Country*?

5 Who played Daisy in *Upstairs Downstairs*?

6 Where did we first meet *Trapper John, M.D.*?

7 What was *Blue Thunder*?

8 Which of the *Girls on Top* appeared in the drama series *Mackenzie*?

9 In *The Sullivans* who plays Grace Sullivan?

10 Where would you find Lt Mike Stone and Det Steve Keller?

11 Who played Grant in *Zodiac*?

12 In *The Six Wives of Henry VIII* who played Anne Boleyn?

Round 7: Science Fiction

1 What was the *Seaview* and where did it go?

2 In which series would you find a computer called Orac?

3 Which family were *Lost in Space*?

4 Which former UNCLE agent 'disappeared' in 1975?

5 Who did Twiki serve in the twenty-fifth century?

6 Lorne Greene swapped the Ponderosa for a spaceship in what?

7 Name the third actor to play Dr Who.

8 Which Nigel Kneale character did Sir John Mills play in 1979?

9 What caused mass blindness in *Day of The Triffids*?

10 In *Star Trek* who is the communications officer?

11 What happened to the moon in *Space 1999*?

12 Name the series in which Ed Bishop played Edward Straker, Commander of SHADO.

GAME 10

1 Which son of a Hollywood legend hosted *The Monte Carlo Show*?

2 Who played Moll Flanders?

3 In *Mission Impossible* what did Barney specialise in?

4 Rock Hudson starred as Col. John Wilder in which mini-series?

5 Who played Madigan?

6 Eddie Booth was married to Joan – who was Bill Reynolds married to?

7 In which series would you find the character Kwai Chang Caine?

8 Which city were Logan 5 and Jessica 6 on the run from?

9 Who presents *Pro-Celebrity Golf*?

10 Sgt Eve Whitfield and Sgt Ed Brown worked for whom?

11 What was *Hollywood Squares* known as in the UK?

12 In *The High Chaparral* who played Victoria de Montoya Cannon?

Round 2: Comedy

1　Who bought Grantley Manor from Audrey Forbes Hamilton?

2　What's happened to Britain in *Comrade Dad*?

3　Name the only two characters to appear in both the first and last episode of *M*A*S*H*?

4　What's *Rhoda*'s surname?

5　Who played Selwyn Froggitt?

6　Who did Mork call every week?

7　Who are Gomez, Morticia, Uncle Fester, Lurch, Grandmama and Thing better known as?

8　Who was the voice of the book in *Hitch-Hiker's Guide to the Galaxy*?

9　Who were *Three of a Kind*?

10　Who was always enquiring if the papers had arrived in *Fawlty Towers*?

11　What was the inspector's catch-phrase in *On The Buses*?

12　In which series did Derek Nimmo, William Mervyn and Robertson Hare poke gentle fun at the clergy?

1 Who were Scooper, Spring, Billie, Brains, Doughnut, Sticks and Tiger?

2 In *Hawaii Five-O* who played Steve McGarrett?

3 Who is Arthur Fonzarelli better known as?

4 Tom Conti played Adam Morris in which cult series?

5 Who was Secret Agent 86?

6 Walter Bingley and Ada Cresswell were the main characters in what?

7 On which show did the Beatles make their American TV debut?

8 Ricardo Montalban and Herve Villechaize played characters on which island?

9 Who was professor of surgery at St Swithin's in *Doctor in the House*?

10 Who was the top operative of *Department S*?

11 Dastardly and Muttley first appeared in which cartoon?

12 Who played ARP Warden Hodges in *Dad's Army*?

From these lists of props identify a television programme:

1 a An army uniform.
   b A map of India.
   c A blonde wig.

2 a A Rolls-Royce.
   b A stethoscope.
   c Two keys to the same flat.

3 a A Norman soldier's helmet.
   b A pair of green tights.
   c A bow and arrow.

4 a A drawing board.
   b A glove puppet.
   c Three handbags.

5 a A union jack waistcoat.
   b Scientific equipment.
   c A giant kitten.

6 a A pair of red boots.
   b A pair of spectacles.
   c A golden lasso.

1   Who was the sheriff of Four Feather Falls?

2   Name Kermit's nephew who was *Half Way up the Stairs*.

3   Who was the *Battery Boy*?

4   Name the presenter who appeared with Muffin the Mule.

5   What did Steve Zodiac command?

6   Which former Goon created the Potties?

7   Who lived between Bill and Ben?

8   Link Hogthrob is the star of which part of the Muppet Show?

9   What was the registration number of Lady Penelope's car?

10 Which two characters sat at the controls of Stingray?

11 Who or what did Captain Scarlet battle with?

12 Name Sooty's girlfriend.

Round 6: General

1 Which ranch was *The Virginian* foreman of?

2 In which series did Ike Godsey run a general store?

3 Who played Natasha in the BBC's serialisation of *War and Peace*?

4 Who ends his show by singing in a rocking chair?

5 What did the American quiz *Tic Tac Dough* become on British TV?

6 Who do the characters in *Taxi* work for?

7 Who would Sylvester the cat like to make a meal of?

8 Who plays Mr Sulu in *Star Trek*?

9 Which cops does Huggy Bear lend a helping hand to?

10 Name the hosts of *The Television Show*.

11 Who played *The Bionic Woman*?

12 Name the film critic who presented *Omnibus*.

Name the private eyes played by these actors:

1 James Garner.

2 David Janssen.

3 Bruce Willis.

4 Cybill Shepherd.

5 William Conrad.

6 Jim Hutton.

7 Richard Roundtree.

8 Alfred Burke.

9 Trevor Eve.

10 Nicholas Ball.

11 Stacey Keach.

12 George Peppard.

GAME 11

1 Which smooth-talking actor played Raffles?

2 Who was Vince's brother in *Just Good Friends*?

3 Name the presenter of *Top Secret*.

4 Who were the two stars of *My Good Woman*?

5 Who played Bill Brand?

6 Name the chairman of *Call My Bluff*.

7 Which impressionist stars in *Now – Something Else*?

8 Who played Sid James's wife in *Bless This House*?

9 Who was Budgie's girlfriend?

10 Which one-time *Tomorrow's World* presenter hosted *Screen Test*?

11 What did the Tripods fit to humans?

12 Who played Mr and Mrs Larkin in *The Larkins*?

Who sang the theme song to these TV programmes:

1 *Champion the Wonder Horse.*
2 *Whatever Happened to the Likely Lads?*
3 *Moonlighting.*
4 *Only Fools and Horses.*
5 *Green Acres.*
6 *Just Good Friends.*
7 *White Horses.*
8 *Hi-De-Hi!*
9 *Dad's Army.*
10 *The Dukes of Hazzard.*
11 *Going Straight.*
12 *The Wombles.*

1 Name the star of *And Mother Makes Three*.

2 Which former professional cricketer became a presenter of *Saturday Night at the Mill*?

3 Who posed the questions on *Ask the Family*?

4 Which cartoon character had a sidekick called Squiddly Diddly?

5 Who was the poetess who shot to fame on *Opportunity Knocks*?

6 Which comedy show came from *Dawson Control*?

7 Max Baer Jnr played Jethro in which American comedy?

8 Who played Barney Miller?

9 What job did Ben Casey do?

10 Who is Barbara Bel Geddes better known as?

11 Alan Bates played *The Mayor of* . . .

12 Which actor played the murderous doctor in *Malice Aforethought*?

From the props listed below identify a television programme:

1   a A baby grand piano.
    b A gold disc.
    c A bust of Beethoven.

2   a A surf board.
    b An American 'black and white' police car.
    c An Hawaiian shirt.

3   a A motorbike and sidecar.
    b A ticket machine
    c A London bus.

4   a A cash register.
    b A delivery boy's bicycle.
    c A Morris Minor.

5   a A box of magic tricks.
    b The 'Kitchener' poster that says 'Your country needs you'.
    c A 1918 theatre programme.

6   a A rosary.
    b A table set for five.
    c A giro from the Liverpool DHSS.

1. Who's the early riser who's convinced his father was Hungarian?

2. Who was Rea married to in *Butterflies*?

3. What was Steptoe's horse called?

4. Who shared a cell with Fletcher?

5. When Tony and Sid shared a house who was their 'char'?

6. Who owned a cat called Vienna?

7. Who was in charge of the Motor Pool at Fort Baxter?

8. In which show would you find Mrs Lumsden?

9. Name the men behind Big Jim Jehosafat and Fat Belly Jones.

10. Who played *Rosie*?

11. Name the town that *Dad's Army* defended.

12. Freddie Frinton and Thora Hird were the stars of what?

1 Who played *The Good Doctor Bodkin Adams*?

2 Dai Francis, Tony Mercer and John Boulter were all what?

3 Who was the comedy star of *Bloomers*?

4 What was odd about the play *Blue Remembered Hills*?

5 Which toupee-wearing ITN newscaster had pronunciation problems?

6 Who presented the series *Botanic Man*?

7 On *Rowan's and Martin's Laugh-In*, who was the 'sock it to me' girl?

8 Name the former BBC announcer who presents *Wish You Were Here*.

9 *Who played Charles Ryder's father in Brideshead Revisited*?

10 Which cricket 'link man' hosted *Come Dancing*?

11 In *Dallas* who plays Cliff Barnes?

12 Who was the long-time front man of *World of Sport*?

Match the *catchphrase* with the correct person.

1	Bob Monkhouse.	a	Don't be a plonker all your life.
2	Bruce Forsyth.		I'm free.
3	Norman Vaughan.	b	
4	Ken Dodd.	c	You scouse git!
5	Dick Emery.	d	So it's goodnight from me – and it's goodnight from him.
6	Del Boy.		
7	Spike Dixon.	e	She knows, you know.
8	John Inman.	f	These are the jokes folks.
9	Hilda Baker.		
10	Alf Garnett.	g	Evening all.
11	The Two Ronnies.	h	Bernie, the bolt.
12	George Dixon.	i	If I can shove in my four penn'th.
		j	Oo – you are awful, but I like you.
		k	Nice to see you, to see you nice.
		l	How tickled I am.

GAME 12

Round 1: General

1 Which spaceship did Captain Christopher Pike once command?

2 Who presents *Saturday Review*?

3 Which character does Nick Berry play in *Eastenders*?

4 Why was *Juliet Bravo* so called?

5 Who succeeded Harry Carpenter as presenter of *Sports Night*?

6 Who is Diahann Carroll's character in *Dynasty*?

7 In *Last of the Summer Wine* what was Foggy's army rank?

8 In which drama series did 'The Mendip Mast' figure?

9 Name the presenter of *The Golden Oldie Picture Show*.

10 Which arts programme does Melvyn Bragg edit?

11 Who's the PM in *Yes, Prime Minister*?

12 Which dolphin had his own series?

1 Who was Worzel Gummidge's girlfriend?

2 Which former Beatle narrates *Thomas the Tank Engine*?

3 What was the first *Blue Peter* dog called?

4 Name the main children's BBC linkman.

5 Who created *Grange Hill*?

6 Which cartoon dog had a master called Shaggy?

7 Susan Stranks co-presented which twice-weekly magazine?

8 What did *T.I.S.W.A.S.* stand for?

9 Name the Richmal Crompton character played on TV by Dennis Waterman.

10 Who are the Flintstones' neighbours?

11 On which programme does Humpty appear?

12 Leslie Crowther and Peter Glaze teamed up on what?

Round 3: General

1   Who did Fran Belding work for?

2   Who are the two main presenters of *Watchdog*?

3   Which couple had *Late Expectations*?

4   Which daytime show is hosted by Pattie Coldwell?

5   What was David Main's profession in *The Main Chance*?

6   What is Peter O'Sullivan famous for?

7   Who played the title role in *Lord Tramp*?

8   Who hosted *Do They Mean Us*?

9   Who kept the women prisoners in *Tenko*?

10 In which TV series did Lulu play a Midlands mum?

11 Which poet told the tale of *Metroland*?

12 What are the pies full of in *Pie in the Sky*?

From the props listed below identify a television programme:

1 a A crucifix.
   b A prayer shawl.
   c A newly tailored gent's suit.

2 a A battered suit.
   b A telescope.
   c A map of the moon.

3 a A Queen Anne table.
   b A Chippendale chair.
   c A Wedgwood plate.

4 a A BBC paper cup.
   b A cabbage.
   c A pencil.

5 a A stopwatch.
   b A greasy pole.
   c A pair of size 27 shoes.

6 a A pink car.
   b A pair of sunglasses.
   c A sign to 'The Cave'.

Name the presenter of these documentary series:

1 *The Ascent of Man.* ✓
2 *Life on Earth.* ✓
3 *The Christians.* ✓
4 *Civilisation.*
5 *Royal Heritage.*
6 *Connections.*
7 *America.* ✓
8 *In Search of the Trojan War.*
9 *Ireland: A Television History.*
10 *The Visit.*
11 *Automania.*
12 *Vikings.*

1 Name the presenter of the documentary series *The First Eden*.

2 Which Scots weatherman takes his shoes off to appear on TV?

3 Who plays Leon in *Escape from Sobibor*?

4 On whose books is the series *One By One* based?

5 Name the Farnon brothers in *All Creatures Great and Small*.

6 What was Barlow's rank in *Z Cars*?

7 Victor Sylvester and Patti Morgan presented which programme?

8 Who plays J. R. Ewing III in *Dallas*?

9 Jean Marsh helped create, and starred in, which series?

10 What was Napoleon Solo's UNCLE number?

11 What was *The Tomorrow People*'s computer called?

12 Who played *Captain Zep – Space Detective*?

Round 7: Military Drama

1 Which number M.A.S.H. unit featured in the long-running series?

2 Name the series about the Royal Flying Corps in World War I.

3 Ali Macgraw and Jan-Michael Vincent starred in which epic war series?

4 Who played Private Schultz?

5 *The Regiment* starred a British actor now seen in *Dynasty* – name him.

6 Vic Morrow and Rick Jason were two stars of which US war series?

7 Which World War I serial was written by Alan Bleasedale?

8 Bernard Hepton played the commandant of what?

9 Where was *Enemy at the Door* set?

10 In which series did HMS *Hero* appear?

11 On which drama series is *'Allo 'Allo!* based?

12 Who was the star of *Wallenberg: A Hero's Story*?

GAME 13

1   In *Moonlighting*, what was the name of David Addison's ex-wife?

2   In the *Mary Tyler Moore Show*, who did Cloris Leachman play?

3   In *Bewitched*, in which town did Darrin and Samantha live?

4   Who joined *TV-am* to temporarily replace Anne Diamond?

5   Who presents *Sweethearts*?

6   Which show does Jancis Robinson present?

7   Who goes *Through the Keyhole*?

8   Who took over as laird from Elizabeth Cunningham in *Take the High Road*?

9   Which detective is played by Fred Dryer?

10   Which game is hosted by Bernie Winters?

11   Who does Mela White play in *Bergerac*?

12   Who starred as Lord Peter Wimsey when Harriet Walker was Harriet Vane?

Round 2: Comedy

1 Who play the two waitresses in *'Allo 'Allo!*?

2 What did the *Magnificent Evans* do for a living?

3 Name the writers of *Hi-De-Hi!*

4 What problem did all the men share in *I Woke Up One Morning*?

5 'There's a lot of it about' – according to whom?

6 In *Dear John* what job did John do?

7 Which actor played the newspaper owner and editor in *Hot Metal*?

8 Name the two stars of *Moody and Pegg*.

9 What did Frank and Betty call their little girl?

10 Which newspaper readers did Jasper Carrott bait on *Carrott's Lib*?

11 When John Cleese played Sherlock Holmes, who played Watson?

12 Where was Eric Idle's weekend television station?

Round 3: General

1 In *Chance In A Million*, what does Tom's girlfriend do for a living?

2 What is *Rumpole of the Bailey*'s address?

3 Who hosts the trivia quiz on *Fax*?

4 Whose secretary is Ethel Ledbetter?

5 Who plays Billy Corkhill in *Brookside*?

6 Who owned Mr Ed?

7 Where do all the contestants stand in *The Price Is Right*?

8 In which show would you have found the Fil Rouge?

9 Who played *A. J. Wentworth B.A.*?

10 What were the first names of Dr Who's first 'companions' from Earth?

11 Which former *Nationwide* presenter reads the *Six O'Clock News*?

12 What was the name of the airline in *Airline*?

From the props listed below identify a television programme:

3 1   a A large boulder.
     b A dinosaur steak.
     c A dog bowl marked 'Dino'.

2 2   a A phaser gun.
     b A pocket 'communicator'.
     c A large book marked 'Captain's log'.

2 3   a A bag of jelly babies.
     b A long multi-coloured scarf.
     c An old blue police box.

3 4   a A pair of yellow checked trousers.
     b A roadsign to 'Nutwood'.
     c A pair of white boots.

1 5   a A map.
     b A bookcase.
     c A helicopter.

1 6   a An *Oxford English Dictionary*.
     b A bell.
     c A pink bow tie.

Round 5: Light Entertainment and Variety Shows

1 Kathy Kaye was a resident singer with whose band?

2 Who sang and painted on his show?

3 Who was a regular guest on Cliff Richard's TV show?

4 Who fixes it?

5 Leslie Crowther, Sheila Burnett and Peter Gordino were three members of what?

6 Which mild-mannered Irishman was in the original *Game for a Laugh* team?

7 Which 'Carry On' star hosted *International Cabaret*?

8 Where did we 'look at the old scoreboard'?

9 Who did Lennie Bennett team up with for a while?

10 On which show is Ali Bongo 'programme associate'?

11 Who hosted *Live from Her Majesty's*?

12 Who provides vocal backing when Benny Hill sings?

Round 6: General

1   Who played Walter in *Emmerdale Farm*?

2   What was the name of the dog Benny rescued in *Crossroads*?

3   Who was the original cleaner at The Rovers Return?

4   Name Tom Chance's girlfriend in *Chance In A Million*.

5   Which former *Young One* starred in *Roll Over Beethoven*?

6   Which comedy series features Fitz and John?

7   Who hosted Channel 4's *The Other Side Of The Tracks*?

8   Which actor did Anthony Hamilton replace in *Cover Up*?

9   Who originally co-hosted *Surprise, Surprise* with Cilla Black?

10 Who was the journalist hero of the drama which launched *Max Headroom*?

11 In which series would you find Nathan Spring?

12 Who plays Taggart?

Name the missing television partners:

1 Sid Little.

2 Hawkeye.

3 Tim Brooke-Taylor, Graeme Garden.

4 Schnorbitz.

5 Mary Beth Lacey.

6 Bootsie.

7 Felix Unger.

8 Musky.

9 Doyle.

10 Makepeace.

11 Boss Hogg.

12 Dick Dastardly.

GAME 14

Round 1: General

1 What was the name of the *Bionic Woman*?

2 Name Iain Cuthbertson's character in *Supergran*.

3 Who hosts *The Newly-Wed Game*?

4 What does W.A.C. stand for?

5 Which TV talent contest was won by Lenny Henry and Marti Caine?

6 On which regional TV news programme did Anne Diamond make her debut?

7 Where in America do the *Golden Girls* live?

8 Who played Bosley in *Charlie's Angels*?

9 Who's *Remington Steele*'s female sidekick?

10 Which afternoon quiz show is hosted by Richard Whiteley?

11 How many husbands named Tanner did Elsie Tanner have?

12 In which series did James Bolam play Jack Ford?

Round 2: *Brookside*

1 What was special about the Jacksons' two sons?

2 What is Billy Corkhill's trade?

3 What sort of business is Gordon Collins involved with?

4 How many children do the Grants have?

5 What was the first name of Heather's first husband?

6 Which actress played Heather?

7 Who left her house to Marie and her other sister?

8 What was taken by Tommy McArdle from the warehouse where George Jackson fought the fire?

9 What sort of business do Pat and Terry run?

10 In the early episodes of the series, what was on the front lawn outside Petra's house?

11 Why did the Collins family move to the Close?

12 On whose estate was Brookside Close built?

1 What was Jim Phelps head of in *Mission Impossible*?

2 Which 'Monkee' started his TV life as *Circus Boy*?

3 'You shall have a fishy, on a little dishy. . . . ' – When?

4 What was *The Price* about?

5 Who was television's *Tarzan*?

6 Which programme was also known as '*TW3*'?

7 Who provided the voice for Fred Flintstone?

8 Clarence the cross-eyed lion appeared in which series?

9 What were Polly James and Nerys Hughes?

10 Who did Leonard Nimoy play in *Mission Impossible*?

11 Who was Hadleigh?

12 What did Wile E. Coyote never manage to catch?

From the props listed below identify a television programme:

1 a A guitar.
  b A small suit.
  c A big suit.

2 a An encyclopedia.
  b A Viking helmet.
  c A black leather chair.

3 a A pair of sunglasses.
  b A copy of *Vogue*.
  c Two detectives' permits.

4 a A Fulham Football Club scarf.
  b A blue denim jacket.
  c A crate stamped 'C. Endell Enterprises'.

5 a A pair of wellies.
  b A black bag.
  c A map of Yorkshire.

6 a A plate of Chinese food.
  b A ten-gallon hat.
  c A sign to 'Virginia City'.

Round 5: *Eastenders*

1 Who runs the launderette?

2 Who is Vicky's real father?

3 What was the name of Ali and Sue's son?

4 Where did Jan and Angie and Den accidentally meet up on holiday?

5 What big lie did Angie tell to try to hold on to Den?

6 What was the name of Lou's husband?

7 Who does Amerjit Deu play?

8 Which London borough is the series set in?

9 Why was Dot Cotton in court?

10 What chronic illness does Lofty suffer from?

11 What kind of machine does Kathy Beale use in her living room?

12 What does Carmel do for a living?

Round 6: General

1 What do the Gummi Bears like to drink?

2 Which family often appeared on *Stars on Sunday*?

3 Which daytime show is hosted by Margo MacDonald?

4 Who shares Grand Prix race commentary with Murray Walker?

5 Which comedy series featured Helen Lederer and Bermuda Triangle?

6 Who made his name on TV as a steeplejack?

7 In which comedy series would you find cousins Balki and Larry?

8 Who is Cagney and Lacey's boss?

9 Name Valerie Harper's character in *Valerie*?

10 From where is *Wogan* broadcast?

11 Who is the BBC's commentator for ice skating?

12 Who makes *Wonderful Wooden Toys*?

Round 7: Cartoons

1 Who is Dudley Do-Right's sworn enemy?

2 What is Scooby Doo?

3 Which cartoon characters live in Jellystone National Park?

4 Who is the police officer in *Top Cat*?

5 Who are the mice hated by Mr Jinx?

6 In which kind of race would you find the Ant Hill Mob?

7 Which all-American hero is supported by his faithful Eagles?

8 If the cartoon family of the past was the Flintstones, what is the family of the future called?

9 What sort of creature is Wattoo-Wattoo?

10 Which firm does Fred Flintstone work for?

11 Which series features a group of youngsters searching for lost civilisations in South America?

12 How old is Max the Mouse?

ANSWERS

Game 1   Round 1
1 *The Mississippi*.   2 Visitors – from outer space.
3 *Mrs King*.   4 One was a convict, the other a judge.
5 *The A-Team*.   6 Jim Bowen hosts *Bullseye* and
appeared in a straight acting role in *Muck and Brass*.
7 Simon Williams.   8 Adam Dalgleish.   9 *The Tripods*.
10 Jane Lapotaire.   11 He died in a fire.   12 The Scott/
Amundsen race to the South Pole.

Game 1   Round 2
1 *Juke Box Jury*.   2 *Oh Boy*.   3 Mike Read.
4 *Ayshea*.   5 Manchester.   6 Janice Nicholls.
7 Peter Cook.   8 Noel Edmonds.   9 *Disc-A-Go-Go*.
10 Jools Holland.   11 Pete Murray.   12 *The Golden Oldie
Picture Show*.

Game 1   Round 3
1 Archie Bunker.   2 Robert Robinson.   3 Tom Baker.
4 Nick Ross.   5 Debbie Rix.   6 Bisley.   7 A van.
8 A bistro.   9 *One By One*.   10 The Showcase
Showdown.   11 Devon Miles.   12 *Horses*.

Game 1   Round 4
1 Peggy, the chalet maid from *Hi-De-Hi!*.   2 The Major,
from *Fawlty Towers*.   3 Parker, Lady Penelope's
butler/chauffeur in *Thunderbirds*.   4 *Adam Adamant*.
5 *Bergerac*.   6 Captain Mainwaring, from *Dad's Army*.

Game 1   Round 5
1 A lion.   2 A rabbit.   3 A frog.   4 An owl.   5 Hedgehog,
mouse and rabbit.   6 A panda.   7 A fox.   8 A gerbil.
9 A cow.   10 Pigs.   11 A dragon.   12 A kitten.

Game 1 Round 6

1 Derek Hobson. 2 Anneka Rice. 3 Anthony Sher.
4 Steve Nallon. 5 Princess Diana of Paradise Island.
6 Grasshopper. 7 *The Champions*. 8 The Federation.
9 Bligh Construction. 10 Margaret Lockwood.
11 Kate. 12 Robert Prosky.

Game 1 Round 7

1 Publican. 2 M.P. 3 Rag and bone man.
4 Policeman. 5 Musician/singer. 6 Spy.
7 Police sergeant. 8 Time Lord. 9 Accountant.
10 Teacher. 11 Television researcher. 12 Superstar.

Game 2 Round 1

1 Joan Van Ark. 2 Solly. 3 David Copperfield. 4 Bill
Buckley. 5 Magnus Magnusson. 6 *Flamingo Road*.
7 Their '*Favourite Things*'. 8 Ted Lowe. 9 Charlie
Hungerford. 10 A *Blankety Blank* cheque book and
pen. 11 *Nice Work*. 12 New York, Paris, Peckham.

Game 2 Round 2

1 *Strong Medicine*. 2 Dennis Potter. 3 Jason
Robards. 4 Shirley Conran. 5 Elizabeth Taylor.
6 *Salem's Lot*. 7 *Bare Essence*. 8 Faye Dunaway.
9 James Smillie. 10 Orson Welles. 11 *Mistral's
Daughter*. 12 Blackie.

Game 2 Round 3

1 At his hospital bedside. 2 Adam Adamant. 3 Jack
Rosenthal. 4 *The Lovers*. 5 Joan Rivers. 6 William
Mervyn. 7 Both starred Mel Smith. 8 Albert Memorial
Hospital. 9 Loudon Wainwright III. 10 Patricia
Hayes. 11 You were gonged! 12 Trapper.

Game 2 Round 4

1 Rigsby, from *Rising Damp*. 2 Mandy, Dick Emery's 'Oo
you are awful' character. 3 Leonard Sachs, the
chairman from *The Good Old Days*. 4 J. R. Ewing.
5 Martin, from *Ever Decreasing Circles*. 6 Harry
Truscott, from *Fairly Secret Army*.

Game 2   Round 5
1 Liverpool.   2 New York.   3 Hartley.
4 Amsterdam.   5 New Town.   6 Holby.   7 Birmingham.
8 Liverpool.   9 Darrowby.   10 Tannochbrae.
11 Tilling.   12 Torquay.

Game 2   Round 6
1 On *Bullseye*.   2 A printing works.   3 Tim
Brooke-Taylor.   4 Mollie Sugden.   5 Carla Lane.   6 Liza
Goddard and Nigel Planer.   7 The Majestics.   8 David
Suchet.   9 His teddy bear.   10 Peter Purves.   11 Paula
Wilcox and Sally Thomsett.   12 He was a cartoonist.

Game 2   Round 7
1 Jeremy Cherfas.   2 *Monkey Business*.   3 Armand
and Michaela Denis.   4 Simon King.   5 David
Attenborough.   6 Sarah Kennedy and Desmond
Morris.   7 *Life on Earth*.   8 David Bellamy.   9 Tony
Soper.   10 Hans and Lotte Hass.   11 Geoffrey
Smith.   12 Jacques Cousteau.

Game 3   Round 1
1 The Blue Moon Detective Agency.   2 Nerys Hughes.   3
Susan.   4 Mrs Goggins.   5 A frog.
6 Zoonie.   7 *Oh Brother*.   8 *The Brothers*.   9 Sir
Kenneth Clark.   10 David Jason.   11 *It's a Knockout*.
12 Servalan.

Game 3   Round 2
1 John Freeman's *Face to Face*.   2 Pamela
Armstrong.   3 *What's on Wogan*.   4 Michael
Parkinson.   5 David Frost.   6 Russell Harty. 7 Simon
Dee.   8 *The Seven Deadly Sins*.   9 Tim Rice.
10 *The Last Resort*.   11 *Just a Nimmo*.   12 *Open Air*.

Game 3   Round 3
1 Dick Flashman.   2 The Cunninghams.   3 William
Moore and Mollie Sugden.   4 *Deewarain*.   5 Jeremy
Beadle.   6 A *Catchphrase*.   7 Leonard Parkin.
8 *The Brothers McGregor*.   9 *Relative Strangers*.
10 An old clock repair shop.   11 Endora, played by
Agnes Moorehead.   12 Matt Frewer.

Game 3   Round 4

1 Hilary — Marti Caine's character from the series of the same name.   2 Arthur Dent, from *Hitch-Hiker's Guide to the Galaxy*.   3 Tony Nelson, from *I Dream of Jeannie*. 4 Vince, from *Just Good Friends*.   5 Colonel Henry Blake, from *M*A*S*H*   6 Nora Batty, from *Last of the Summer Wine*.

Game 3   Round 5

1 Humphrey Burton.   2 Andrew Lloyd-Webber. 3 Richard Baker.   4 Raymond Baxter.   5 *Take Nobody's Word For It*.   6 Milton Keynes.   7 Huw Wheldon.   8 Ken Russell.   9 Melvyn Bragg.   10 *Halls of Fame*. 11 *Saturday Review*.   12 *Arena*.

Game 3   Round 6

1 Roger Moore.   2 Antiques.   3 James Ellis – he appeared in both.   4 *The Streets of San Francisco*. 5 Dave.   6 Brigit Forsyth.   7 J 1610.   8 Stoker.   9 David Vine.   10 *Masterteam*.   11 Hattie Jacques.   12 Galton and Simpson.

Game 3   Round 7

1 Snooker.   2 Angling.   3 Motor racing.   4 Football. 5 Cricket.   6 Sailing.   7 Football.   8 Cricket. 9 Sailing.   10 Football.   11 Horse riding.   12 Cricket.

Game 4   Round 1

1 Cut the flowers off.   2 Gus MacDonald.   3 Andy Crawford, in *Dixon of Dock Green*.   4 *Girls in Grey*. 5 Ian Carmichael.   6 In his pen.   7 The Bentinck. 8 John Alderton and Pauline Collins.   9 He was killed in a bomb explosion in *Doomwatch*.   10 Blair General. 11 555 2368.   12 Looby Loo.

Game 4   Round 2

1 Michael Aspel.   2 Kenneth Kendall.   3 Christopher Chataway.   4 Selina Scott.   5 Peter Sissons.   6 Angela Rippon.   7 Big Ben.   8 Kate Adie.   9 Sandy Gall. 10 Gordon Honeycombe.   11 Robert Dougall.   12 Martin Lewis.

Game 4   Round 3
1 The Little Ladies.   2 The Staretts.   3 Alison
Mitchell.   4 He was in the grocery business.   5 A soup
dragon.   6 Susan Hampshire.   7 The Laceys.   8 Jane
Lucas.   9 *The Befrienders*.   10 *Compact*.   11 Eamonn
Andrews.   12 *Bleep and Booster*.

Game 4   Round 4
1 Albert Steptoe, from *Steptoe and Son*.   2 Fozzy
Bear.   3 Del Boy, from *Only Fools and Horses*.
4 Postman Pat.   5 Rumpole of the Bailey.   6 Sergeant
Bilko.

Game 4   Round 5
1 Brownlow.   2 Clare Falconbridge.   3 Amy Turtle.
4 He was a newspaper editor.   5 Charlie Mycroft.
6 1975.   7 Sandy Richardson.   8 Kings Oak.   9 Mrs
Babbitt.   10 Vince.   11 Tommy Lancaster.   12 Debbie.

Game 4   Round 6
1 *Knight Rider*.   2 Sue Robbie.   3 *E.R.*   4 The Big
Guy.   5 Dr Cameron, Dr Finlay and Janet.   6 *Never the
Twain*.   7 *Panorama*.   8 A mouse.   9 *The Good
Word*.   10 Mrs Scrubbitt.   11 He was his nephew.
12 The Sandwich Quiz.

Game 4   Round 7
1 The Bellamys.   2 *Neighbours*.   3 The Clampetts.
4 The Stevens.   5 The Laceys.   6 The Beales.
7 The Pains.   8 The Keatons.   9 *Sorry!*   10 *Marriage
Lines*.   11 Harrap.   12 *Only Fools and Horses*.

Game 5   Round 1
1 Lucy Bates.   2 *All in Good Faith*.   3 *La Dépêche*.
4 Herbert Viola.   5 *A Gardener's Calendar* on Channel
4.   6 Frazer Hines and Wendy Padbury.   7 Youth
Enquiry Service.   8 Brackman, Chaney and Kuzack.
9 Car 54.   10 Matthew Parris.   11 Mongy.
12 He was a butcher.

Game 5   Round 2
1 Darius.   2 Mr Valentine.   3 Clayton Farlowe.
4 In a plane crash.   5 A Mercedes.   6 Peter.
7 Jack and Jamie.   8 Chinese.   9 Wes Parmalee.
10 Dusty.   11 Mark Grayson.   12 Mickey.

Game 5   Round 3
1 Harry Stoneham.   2 *Colditz*.   3 Dermot Walsh.   4 Tony
Hancock and Sid James.   5 A virus that killed off most of
the human race.   6 A halo appear above his head.
7 *Sailor*.   8 Isla.   9 Dinsdale Landen.   10 They were
endowed with special powers by Tibetan monks.
11 World War 1.   12 Walter Winchell.

Game 5   Round 4
1 *The Morecambe and Wise Show*.   2 *Cagney and
Lacey*.   3 *The Tom O'Connor Road Show*.   4 *Please
Sir!*   5 *Only Fools and Horses*.   6 *Sorry!*

Game 5   Round 5
1 Braddock.   2 *Flamingo Road*.   3 Rodney
Harrington.   4 *Knotts Landing*.   5 Pamela Sue Martin.
6 *The Mary Tyler Moore Show*.   7 Kirstin Shepard in 1980
– B. J. Calhoun in 1987.   8 *The Winds of War*.   9 *Falcon
Crest* (Jane Wyman was married to Ronald Reagan).
10 Charlton Heston and Barbara Stanwyck.
11 Ray Krebbs and Clayton Farlowe.   12 Harry Andrews.

Game 5   Round 6
1 Dennis Potter.   2 *Crown Court*.   3 Barry Cryer.
4 Bernard Levin.   5 Jonathan King.   6 A robot.   7 *The
Cuckoo Waltz*.   8 Anthony Hopkins.   9 Uncle Buck.
10 Petrocelli.   11 John Hurt.   12 Adolfo Celi.

Game 5   Round 7
1 *The High Chaparral*.   2 Matt Dillon/James Arness.
3 *Branded*.   4 James Drury.   5 Hoss, Little Joe, Adam.
6 Frankie Laine.   7 Scout.   8 Pete Duel and Roger
Davis.   9 Steve McQueen.   10 Bret and Bart – James
Garner and Jack Kelly   11 Major Adams.   12 *The
Adventures of Rin Tin Tin*.

Game 6   Round 1
1 Diane Keen.   2 Arthur.   3 He was a writer.   4 Marius
Goring.   5 Judi Dench and Michael Williams.   6 *Casey
Jones*.   7 *Burke's Law*.   8 *Connie*.   9 Billy Cotton.
10 Undercover agents.   11 Jacques Cousteau.   12 Leslie
Phillips.

Game 6   Round 2
1 *Animal Magic*.   2 *Blue Peter*.   3 *Tales from Europe*.
4 Noel Edmonds.   5 Slowcoach.   6 *The Double
Deckers*.   7 *H. R. Pufnstuf*.   8 Tufty.   9 Desmond
Morris.   10 *The Black Pig*.   11 *Junior Showtime*.
12 *Clapperboard*.

Game 6   Round 3
1 Deputy Dawg.   2 Mrs Overall.   3 *Call My Bluff*.
4 *The Man From Atlantis*.   5 The Ingalls.   6 The Dragon
Club – Olivers.   7 A jeannie.   8 Paul Daneman.
9 *The Multi-Coloured Swap Shop*.   10 Monica Rose.
11 *Search for a Star*.   12 *United*.

Game 6   Round 4
1 Worzel Gummidge.   2 Hadleigh.   3 Private Schulz.
4 Lord Peter Wimsey.   5 Ethel from *Eastenders*.
6 Bert Lynch from *Z Cars*.

Game 6   Round 5
1 Skaro.   2 The Ice Warriors.   3 Jelly babies.   4 Dr Who's
car.   5 Ian and Barbara.   6 A recorder.   7 Sonic.   8 They
were both the doctor.   9 One of the keys of Marinus.
10 The Web Planet.   11 Peter Purves.   12 K9.

Game 6   Round 6
1 Carmen Silvera.   2 *Lost in Space*.   3 Shirley
Cheriton.   4 *Highway*.   5 John Mortimer.   6 *Danger
U.X.B.*   7 Lifted his arm and leg and had fun with his
reflection.   8 Manuel's pet rat.   9 Jack Haig.   10 *Driving
Ambition*.   11 Harve Smithfield.   12 Mogul.

Game 6 Round 7
1 Minnie Caldwell. 2 Lucille. 3 She was electrocuted while using a hair-dryer. 4 Florrie Lindley. 5 Emily Nugent. 6 The Mission Hall. 7 Ray Langton. 8 He was shot. 9 Betty Driver. 10 To live abroad. 11 Bernard Youens. 12 Newton and Ridley.

Game 7 Round 1
1 Ned Sherrin. 2 Senna, the soothsayer in *Up Pompeii*. 3 Tom Selleck. 4 Johnny Ball. 5 Scotty. 6 Dave. 7 Blue string pudding. 8 Madame (Cholet). 9 Dr Johnny Fever. 10 Roland – he helped revive *TV-am*'s fortunes. 11 Cloris Leachman. 12 It lit up.

Game 7 Round 2
1 Charles Dance. 2 Tony Bell. 3 George. 4 Mr Waverly. 5 Computer fraud. 6 *The Girl from UNCLE*. 7 Alan Bates. 8 Clannad. 9 *The Beiderbecke Affair*. 10 Mark Cain. 11 *Edge of Darkness*. 12 Patrick McGoohan.

Game 7 Round 3
1 A customised dragster hearse. 2. Graham Kerr. 3 Jim Backus – the voice of *Mr Magoo* and a castaway on the island. 4 Jellystone. 5 Mr Roarke. 6 Jean Anderson. 7 Cleopatra. 8 The Delta Rho. 9 The Woolpack. 10 Bruce Forsyth, Larry Grayson and Roy Castle. 11 Selina Scott. 12 Katie Boyle.

Game 7 Round 4
1 *Bill and Ben, the Flowerpot Men*. 2 *Late Starter*. 3 *The Singing Detective*. 4 *Shoestring*. 5 *Maigret*. 6 *Tutti Frutti*.

Game 7 Round 5
1 Hughie Green. 2 Alan Taylor. 3 Kenny Everett, then Lance Percival. 4 Max Bygraves. 5 *My Music*. 6 *What's My Line*? 7 *Mastermind*. 8 Michael Barrymore. 9 Anne Aston. 10 Take the money. 11 Lennie Bennett. 12 *Sale of the Century*.

Game 7 Round 6

1 Robert Davies. 2 Georgina Hale. 3 Three – Loretta Swit, Meg Foster and Sharon Gless. 4 *You and Me*. 5 Sir Basil and Lady Rosemary, in *The Herbs*. 6 Hugh, Pugh, Barney, McGrew, Cuthbert, Dibble and Grub. 7 On a scooter. 8 *The Tomorrow People*. 9 Admiral Nelson. 10 The Aquaphibians. 11 Pamela. 12 John Cleese.

Game 7 Round 7

1 Andrew Cruickshank. 2 Richard Chamberlain. 3 Jack Klugman. 4 Peter Davison. 5 Barbara Flynn. 6 Larry Linville. 7 Raymond Massey. 8 Freddie Jones. 9 Ben Cross. 10 Mike Farrell. 11 Bill Simpson. 12 Robert Young.

Game 8 Round 1

1 Joan Miller. 2 John Pitman and Esther Rantzen. 3 Noah Beery, the avuncular American actor, starred in both. 4 The headmaster, Algy Herries. 5 Leonard Sachs. 6 Colin Crompton and Bernard Manning. 7 Ben Vereen. 8 *Lytton's Diary*. 9 Mrs Thursday. 10 *Westminster*. 11 John Lennon. 12 Hill's Angels.

Game 8 Round 2

1 *Compact*. 2 Leo and Lynne. 3 Patrick Wymark. 4 Gabrielle Drake. 5 Minnie Caldwell. 6 St Angela's. 7 *Emergency Ward Ten*. 8 Walford United. 9 Alan Browning. 10 Joe Sugden. 11 Liverpool. 12 They are both dogs in *Eastenders*.

Game 8 Round 3

1 Deborah Kerr, Jenny Seagrove. 2 Ray's mother, Margaret. 3 Starsky's. 4 Dutch. 5 He was a defence lawyer. 6 Alan Whicker. 7 *One Man and His Dog*. 8 Bob Harris. 9 Jimmy Savile. 10 *The Saint*. 11 Tony Randall and Jack Klugman. 12 *Now get out of That*.

Game 8 Round 4

1 Kojak. 2 Columbo. 3 Miss Marple. 4 The Lone Ranger. 5 Angie, from *Eastenders*. 6 Compo, from *Last of the Summer Wine*.

Game 8   Round 5
1 Tennis.   2 Athletics.   3 Football.   4 Snooker.
5 Darts.   6 Equestrian events.   7 Athletics.   8 Wrestling.
9 Darts.   10 Athletics.   11 Rugby Union.   12 Football.

Game 8   Round 6
1 Orson Welles.   2 *Name That Tune*.   3 Robert Vaughn,
Nyree Dawn Porter, Tony Anholt.   4 *McMillan and
Wife*.   5 Selina Scott and Jeff Banks.   6 Angie
Dickinson.   7 He bent it in half on *Blankety Blank*.
8 *Odd One Out*.   9 *The Andy Williams Show*.   10 *Going
for a Song*.   11 *Nancy*.   12 He was in a helicopter
accident.

Game 8   Round 7
1 *Cheers*.   2 Danny De Vito.   3 *F-Troop*.   4 The
Clampetts.   5 He dressed in women's clothes in order to
get discharged from the army.   6 Lucille Ball.   7 Robert
Guillaume.   8 She's a waitress.   9 Magical powers.
10 Fort Baxter.   11 *WKRP in Cincinnati*.   12 Dick Van
Dyke. He was a scriptwriter.

Game 9   Round 1
1 *Pass The Buck*.   2 The Doozers.   3 The Jolly Theatre
School.   4 El Puerco.   5 Robert McCall.   6 *Constant
Hot Water*.   7 *No. 73*.   8 Alexis.   9 He was killed in a car
crash.   10 *Dempsey and Makepeace*.   11 *The Trap
Door*.   12 Covert Activities, Thames Section.

Game 9   Round 2
1 Fred Astaire.   2 Raymond Francis.   3 They both
played women inspectors in *Juliet Bravo*.   4 Peter
Byrne.   5 Carter, in *The Sweeney*.   6 Miss Marple.
7 Barry Morse.   8 *The Untouchables*.   9 Hawaii.
10 *Z Cars*.   11 *Baretta*.   12 *Highway Patrol*.

Game 9   Round 3
1 *The Six Million Dollar Man*.   2 Shari Lewis.   3 He was
an undercover cop.   4 *Search*.   5 Scooby Doo.
6 Marlon Brando.   7 *Ripping Yarns*.   8 Groutie.   9 Two
astronauts on *Planet of the Apes*.   10 He sold sheet
music.   11 Della Street.   12 *The Partridge Family*.

Game 9 Round 4
1 Terry, from *Minder* 2 Oz, from *Auf Wiedersehen Pet*. 3 Alf Garnett. 4 Gladys Pugh, from *Hi-De-Hi!* 5 Rumpole. 6 Rodney, from *Only Fools And Horses*.

Game 9 Round 5
1 Keith Michell. 2 Soames Forsyte. 3 Duke Street. 4 Casanova. 5 *Poldark*. 6 Glenda Jackson. 7 Timothy West. 8 Eaton Place. 9 Roger Rees. 10 Anthony Hopkins. 11 *Shogun*. 12 Borgia.

Game 9 Round 6
1 Alexandra Palace. 2 Angela Rippon. 3 *The Morecambe and Wise Show*. 4 Susan Penhaligon. 5 Jacqueline Tong. 6 *M*A*S*H* 7 A technically ultra-sophisticated helicopter. 8 Tracy Ullman. 9 Lorraine Bayly. 10 On *the Streets of San Francisco*. 11 Anton Rodgers. 12 Dorothy Tutin.

Game 9 Round 7
1 A submarine on a *Voyage to the Bottom of the Sea*. 2 *Blake's Seven*. 3 The Robinsons. 4 David McCallum – he played the invisible man. 5 Buck Rogers. 6 *Battlestar Galactica*. 7 Jon Pertwee. 8 Prof. Quatermass. 9 A dazzling meteor shower. 10 Lieutenant Uhura. 11 It was blown out of orbit and floated off into space. 12 *U.F.O.*

Game 10 Round 1
1 Patrick Wayne. 2 Julia Foster. 3 Electronics. 4 *The Martian Chronicles*. 5 Richard Widmark. 6 Barbie – in *Love Thy Neighbour*. 7 *Kung Fu*. 8 The City of Domes. 9 Peter Alliss. 10 Chief Ironside. 11 *Celebrity Squares*. 12 Linda Cristal.

Game 10   Round 2
1 Richard De Vere.   2 It's been invaded by Russians.
3 Captain Benjamin Franklin 'Hawkeye' Pierce and Major
Margaret 'Hotlips' Houlihan.   4 Morgenstern.   5 Bill
Maynard.   6 Orson.   7 *The Addams Family*.   8 Peter
Jones.   9 Lenny Henry, Tracy Ullman and David
Copperfield.   10 Major Gowen.   11 'I hate you,
Butler'.   12 *All Gas and Gaiters*.

Game 10   Round 3
1 *The Double Deckers*.   2 Jack Lord.   3 The Fonz.
4 *The Glittering Prizes*.   5 Maxwell Smart in *Get Smart*.
6 *For the Love of Ada*.   7 *The Ed Sullivan Show*.
8 *Fantasy Island* – Mr Roarke and Tattoo.   9 Sir Geoffrey
Loftus.   10 Jason King.   11 *The Wacky Races*.   12 Bill
Pertwee.

Game 10   Round 4
1 *It Ain't Half Hot Mum*.   2 *Don't Wait Up*.   3 *Robin
Hood*.   4 *Keep It In The Family*.   5 *The Goodies*.
6 *Wonder Woman*.

Game 10   Round 5
1 Tex Tucker.   2 Robin.   3 Torchy.   4 Annette Mills.
5 *Fireball XL5*.   6 Michael Bentine.   7 Weed.   8 Pigs in
Space.   9 FAB 1.   10 Troy Tempest and Phones.
11 The Mysterons.   12 Soo.

Game 10   Round 6
1 Shiloh.   2 *The Waltons*.   3 Morag Hood.   4 Val
Doonican.   5 *Criss Cross Quiz*.   6 The Sunshine Cab
Company.   7 Tweety Pie.   8 George Takei.   9 *Starsky
and Hutch*.   10 Kieran Prendiville and Fern Britton.
11 Lindsay Wagner.   12 Barry Norman.

Game 10   Round 7
1 Jim Rockford.   2 Harry O.   3 David Addison.
4 Maddie Hayes.   5 Frank Cannon.   6 Ellery Queen.
7 Shaft.   8 Frank Marker.   9 Shoestring.   10 Hazell.
11 Mike Hammer.   12 Banacek.

Game 11   Round 1
1 Anthony Valentine.   2 Cliffie.   3 Barry Took.   4 Sylvia
Syms and Leslie Crowther.   5 Jack Shepherd.   6 Robert
Robinson.   7 Rory Bremner.   8 Diana Coupland.
9 Hazel.   10 Michael Rodd.   11 Caps that dulled certain
senses.   12 Peggy Mount and David Kossoff.

Game 11   Round 2
1 Frankie Laine.   2 Manfred Mann.   3 Al Jarreau.
4 John Sullivan   5 Eddie Albert/Eva Gabor.   6 Paul
Nicholas.   7 Jackie.   8 Paul Shane and the
Yellowcoats.   9 Bud Flanagan.   10 Waylon
Jennings.   11 Ronnie Barker.   12 Mike Batt.

Game 11   Round 3
1 Wendy Craig.   2 Tony Lewis.   3 Robert Robinson.
4 Secret Squirrel.   5 Pam Ayres.   6 *The Dawson
Watch.*   7 *The Beverly Hillbillies.*   8 Hal Linden.
9 He was a doctor.   10 Miss Ellie in *Dallas.*
11 *Casterbridge.*   12 Hywel Bennett.

Game 11   Round 4
1 *Roll over Beethoven.*   2 *Hawaii Five-O.*   3 *On the
Buses.*   4 *Open All Hours.*   5 *Lost Empires.*   6 *Bread.*

Game 11   Round 5
1 Granville in *Open All Hours.*   2 Ben.   3 Hercules.
4 Godber in *Porridge.*   5 Mrs Cravatt/Patricia Hayes.
6 Rigsby in *Rising Damp.*   7 Sergeant Bilko.   8 *Sorry!*
9 Ronnie Corbett and Ronnie Barker.   10 Paul
Greenwood.   11 Warmington on Sea.   12 *Meet the Wife.*

Game 11   Round 6
1 Timothy West.   2 Black and White Minstrels.
3 Richard Beckinsale.   4 Adult actors played children.
5 Reginald Bosanquet.   6 David Bellamy.   7 Judy
Carne.   8 Judith Chalmers.   9 Sir John Gielgud.
10 Peter West.   11 Ken Kercheval.   12 Dickie Davies.

Game 11   Round 7
1h.   2k.   3f.   4l.   5j.   6a.   7i.   8b.
9e.   10c.   11d.   12g.

Game 12   Round 1
1 The USS *Enterprise*.   2 Russell Davies.   3 Wicksy.
4 It was the woman inspector's radio call sign.   5 Steve
Ryder.   6 Dominique.   7 Corporal.   8 *Heart of the
Country*.   9 Dave Lee Travis.   10 *The South Bank Show*.
11 Jim Hacker.   12 Flipper.

Game 12   Round 2
1 Aunt Sally.   2 Ringo Starr.   3 Petra.   4 Phillip
Schofield.   5 Phil Redmond.   6 Scooby Doo.
7 *Magpie*.   8 Today Is Saturday Watch And Smile.
9 *Just William*.   10 Barney and Betty Rubble.
11 *Playschool*.   12 *Crackerjack*.

Game 12   Round 3
1 Chief Ironside.   2 Lynn Faulds Wood and John
Stapleton.   3 Ted and Liz Jackson.   4 *Open Air*.
5 Solicitor.   6 Racing commentary.   7 Hugh Lloyd.
8 Derek Jameson.   9 The Japanese.   10 *The Growing
Pains of Adrian Mole*.   11 Sir John Betjeman.   12 Songs.

Game 12   Round 4
1 *Never Mind the Quality Feel the Width*.   2 *The Sky at
Night*.   3 *The Antiques Roadshow*.   4 *Crackerjack*.
5 *It's a Knockout*.   6 *Roland Rat – The Series*.

Game 12   Round 5
1 Dr Jacob Bronowski.   2 David Attenborough.
3 Bamber Gascoigne.   4 Kenneth Clark.   5 Huw
Wheldon.   6 James Burke.   7 Alistair Cooke.   8 Michael
Wood.   9 Robert Kee.   10 Desmond Wilcox.   11 Julian
Pettifer.   12 Magnus Magnusson.

Game 12   Round 6
1 David Attenborough.   2 Ian McCaskill.   3 Alan
Arkin.   4 David Taylor.   5 Siegfried and Tristan.
6 Detective Inspector.   7 *Television Dancing Club*.
8 Omar Katz.   9 *Upstairs Downstairs*.   10 11.
11 Tim.   12 Paul Greenwood.

Game 12   Round 7
1 The 4077.   2 *Wings*.   3 *The Winds of War*.   4 Michael
Elphick.   5 Christopher Cazonove.   6 *Combat!*
7 *The Monocled Mutineer*.   8 *Colditz*.   9 Guernsey.
10 *Warship*.   11 *Secret Army*.   12 Richard Chamberlain.

Game 13   Round 1
1 Tess.   2 Phyllis.   3 Westport.   4 Caroline Righton.
5 Larry Grayson.   6 *The Wine Programme*.   7 Lloyd
Grossman.   8 Lady Margaret Ross-Gifford.
9 *Hunter*.   10 *Whose Baby?*   11 Diamante Lil.
12 Edward Petherbridge.

Game 13   Round 2
1 Vicki Michelle, Francesca Gonshaw.   2 He was a
photographer.   3 Jimmy Perry and David Croft.
4 Alcoholism.   5 Spike Milligan.   6 Schoolteacher.
7 Robert Hardy.   8 Derek Waring and Judy Cornwell.
9 Jessica.   10 *The Sun*.   11 Arthur Lowe.   12 Rutland.

Game 13   Round 3
1 She's a librarian.   2 25B Foxbury Court, Gloucester
Road, London.   3 Billy Butler.   4 Donald Turner's, in
One By One.   5 John McArdle.   6 Wilbur Post.
7 Contestant's Row.   8 *It's A Knockout*.   9 Arthur
Lowe.   10 Ian and Barbara.   11 Sue Lawley.   12 Ruskin
Airways.

Game 13   Round 4
1 *The Flintstones*.   2 *Star Trek*.   3 *Dr Who*.   4 *Rupert
The Bear*.   5 *Treasure Hunt*.   6 *Call My Bluff*.

Game 13   Round 5
1 Billy Cotton.   2 Rolf Harris.   3 Olivia Newton-John.
4 Jimmy Savile.   5 *The Saturday Crowd*.   6 Henry
Kelly.   7 Kenneth Williams.   8 *The Generation Game*.
9 Jerry Stevens.   10 *The Paul Daniels Magic Show*.
11 Jimmy Tarbuck.   12 The Ladybirds.

Game 13   Round 6
1 Al Dixon.   2 Moses.   3 Martha Longhurst.   4 Alison Little.   5 Nigel Planer.   6 *Relative Strangers*.   7 Paul Gambaccini.   8 Jon-Erik Hexum.   9 Christopher Biggins.   10 Edison Carter.   11 *Star Cops*.   12 Mark McManus.

Game 13   Round 7
1 Eddie Large.   2 Trapper or B.J.   3 Bill Oddie.
4 Bernie Winters.   5 Christine Cagney.   6 Snudge.
7 Oscar Madison.   8 Vince.   9 Bodie.   10 Dempsey.
11 Roscoe Coltrane.   12 Muttley.

Game 14   Round 1
1 Jamie Sommers.   2 Scunner Campbell.   3 Gloria Hunniford.   4 *Wide Awake Club*.   5 *New Faces*.
6 *Points West*.   7 Miami.   8 David Doyle.   9 Laura Holt.   10 *Countdown*.   11 Two.   12 *When the Boat Comes In*.

Game 14   Round 2
1 They were twins.   2 He's an electrician.
3 Antiques.   4 Four.   5 Roger.   6 Amanda Burton.
7 Petra.   8 Cigarettes.   9 A transport firm.   10 A group of old cookers.   11 Paul was made redundant.   12 Lord Derby.

Game 14   Round 3
1 The IMF — Impossible Missions Force.   2 Mickey Dolenz (in *Circus Boy* he was billed as Mickey Braddock).
3 *When the Boat Comes In*.   4 A businessman whose wife was kidnapped by Irish terrorists.   5 Ron Ely.
6 *That Was The Week That Was*.   7 Al Reed.   8 *Daktari*.
9 *The Liver Birds*.   10 Paris.   11 Gerald Harper.
12 The Road Runner.

Game 14   Round 4
1 *The Little and Large Show*.   2 *Mastermind*.
3 *Moonlighting*.   4 *Budgie*.   5 *All Creatures Great and Small*.   6 *Bonanza*.

Game 14   Round 5
1 Pauline Fowler.   2 Den Watts.   3 Hassan.
4 Venice.   5 She said she was dying.   6 Albert.
7 Dr Singh.   8 Walford.   9 She was charged with
shoplifting.   10 Asthma.   11 A knitting machine.
12 She's a health visitor.

Game 14   Round 6
1 Gummi Berry Juice.   2 The Poole Family.   3 *Advice
Shop*.   4 James Hunt.   5 *Hello Mum*.   6 Fred
Dibnah.   7 *Perfect Strangers*.   8 Lieutenant Samuels.
9 Valerie Hogan.   10 The Television Theatre in
Shepherds Bush.   11 Alan Weeks.   12 Richard Blizzard.

Game 14   Round 7
1 Snidley Whiplash.   2 A dog.   3 Yogi Bear and Boo Boo.
4 Officer Dibble.   5 Pixie and Dixie.   6 A Wacky
Race.   7 Roger Ramjet.   8 The Jetsons.   9 A bird from
outer space.   10 The Slaterock Gravel Company.
11 The Mysterious Cities of Gold.   12 2000 years old.